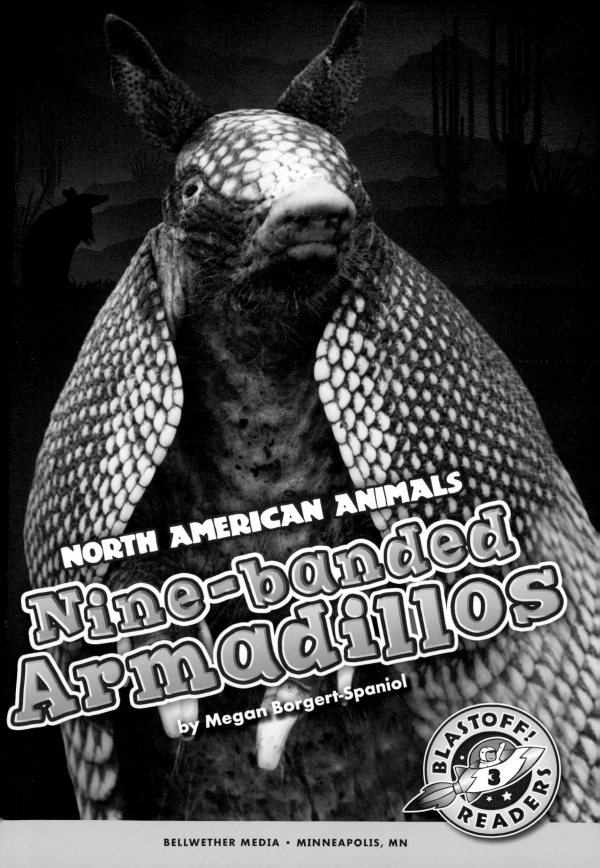

NORTH AMERICAN ANIMALS

Nine-banded Armadillos

by Megan Borgert-Spaniol

BELLWETHER MEDIA • MINNEAPOLIS, MN

Note to Librarians, Teachers, and Parents:

Blastoff! Readers are carefully developed by literacy experts and combine standards-based content with developmentally appropriate text.

Level 1 provides the most support through repetition of high-frequency words, light text, predictable sentence patterns, and strong visual support.

Level 2 offers early readers a bit more challenge through varied simple sentences, increased text load, and less repetition of high-frequency words.

Level 3 advances early-fluent readers toward fluency through increased text and concept load, less reliance on visuals, longer sentences, and more literary language.

Level 4 builds reading stamina by providing more text per page, increased use of punctuation, greater variation in sentence patterns, and increasingly challenging vocabulary.

Level 5 encourages children to move from "learning to read" to "reading to learn" by providing even more text, varied writing styles, and less familiar topics.

Whichever book is right for your reader, Blastoff! Readers are the perfect books to build confidence and encourage a love of reading that will last a lifetime!

This edition first published in 2016 by Bellwether Media, Inc.

No part of this publication may be reproduced in whole or in part without written permission of the publisher. For information regarding permission, write to Bellwether Media, Inc., Attention: Permissions Department, 5357 Penn Avenue South, Minneapolis, MN 55419.

Library of Congress Cataloging-in-Publication Data

Borgert-Spaniol, Megan, 1989- author.
  Nine-banded Armadillos / by Megan Borgert-Spaniol.
    pages cm. – (Blastoff! Readers. North American Animals)
  Summary: "Simple text and full-color photography introduce beginning readers to nine-banded armadillos. Developed by literacy experts for students in kindergarten through third grade"– Provided by publisher.
  Audience: Ages 5-8
  Audience: K to grade 3
  Includes bibliographical references and index.
  ISBN 978-1-62617-261-6 (hardcover: alk. paper)
  1. Nine-banded armadillo–Juvenile literature. 2. Armadillos–Juvenile literature. I. Title.
  QL737.E23B67 2016
  599.3'12–dc23
                                              2015000509

Printed in the United States of America, North Mankato, MN.

Table of Contents

What Are Nine-banded Armadillos?

Nine-banded armadillos are **mammals** with **scales**. They are the only kind of armadillo found in North America.

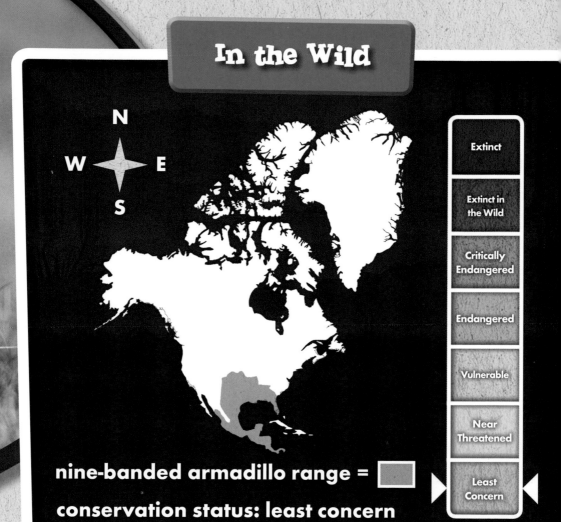

In the Wild

N
W • E
S

Extinct

Extinct in the Wild

Critically Endangered

Endangered

Vulnerable

Near Threatened

Least Concern

nine-banded armadillo range = ▢

conservation status: least concern

They live in warm, wet areas in the southeastern United States and farther south. Forests and **scrublands** are their homes.

Nine-banded armadillos measure about 2.5 feet (0.8 meters) from nose to tail. The tail alone is 1 foot (0.3 meters) long!

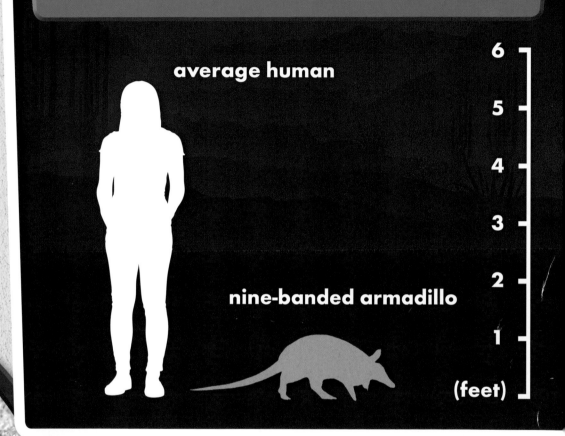

Size of a Nine-banded Armadillo

average human

nine-banded armadillo

6
5
4
3
2
1
(feet)

They are sometimes called long-nosed armadillos because of their face shape.

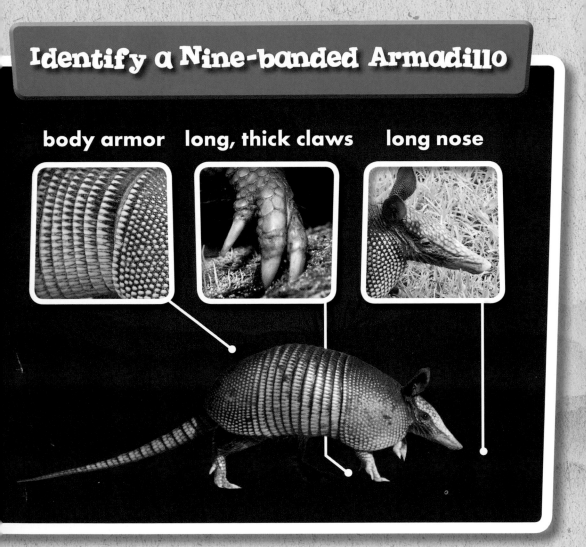

body armor long, thick claws long nose

Nine-banded armadillos are covered in **scutes**. About nine bands of this **armor** cross their backs.

Their bellies are soft and hairy.
The hairs are like wires.

Nine-banded armadillos are **insectivores**. They mainly eat ants, beetles, and other insects.

earthworms

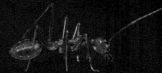

fire ants

yellow jackets

snails

green June beetles

white grubs

They also dig up **grubs**, worms, and snails.

The armadillos sniff the
ground to find **prey**.

They sweep up small insects with their long, sticky tongues. They use their v-shaped teeth to chew larger prey.

Nine-banded armadillos can walk across the bottoms of small streams.

They can also swim in deeper water.
They swallow air to help them float.

Burrows

Nine-banded armadillos dig **burrows** with their strong front claws.

One armadillo often digs several
burrows. It fills the tunnels with
leaves and grasses.

Burrows are used to protect the young. Females give birth to four **pups** in spring. The pups stay safe underground for a few weeks.

Baby Facts

Name for babies:	pups
Size of litter:	4 pups
Length of pregnancy:	7 to 8 months
Time spent with mom:	4 to 6 months

Animals to Avoid

alligators

great horned owls

bobcats

mountain lions

coyotes

black bears

Nine-banded armadillos also run into burrows to escape alligators, black bears, and other **predators**. They hold still and let their armor protect them!

Glossary

armor—a hard covering that protects

burrows—holes or tunnels that some animals dig in the ground

grubs—very young beetles

insectivores—animals that eat mainly insects

mammals—warm-blooded animals that have backbones and feed their young milk

predators—animals that hunt other animals for food

prey—animals that are hunted by other animals for food

pups—baby armadillos; all four pups in a litter look exactly the same.

scales—small plates of skin that cover and protect an armadillo's body

scrublands—lands with short bushes and trees

scutes—bony scales that cover the bodies of some animals

To Learn More

AT THE LIBRARY

Phillips, Dee. *Armadillo's Burrow*. New York, N.Y.: Bearport Publishing, 2013.

Sebastian, Emily. *Armadillos*. New York, N.Y.: PowerKids Press, 2012.

Storad, Conrad J. *Don't Ever Cross That Road!: An Armadillo Story*. Tempe, Ariz.: RGU Group, 2006.

ON THE WEB

Learning more about nine-banded armadillos is as easy as 1, 2, 3.

1. Go to www.factsurfer.com.

2. Enter "nine-banded armadillos" into the search box.

3. Click the "Surf" button and you will see a list of related web sites.

With factsurfer.com, finding more information is just a click away.

Index

The images in this book are reproduced through the courtesy of: Rolf Nussbaumer/ Nature Picture Library, front cover, p. 9; age fotostock/ age fotostock/ Superstock, pp. 4-5; IrinaK, pp. 6-7, 8 (top right); Heiko Kiera, p. 8 (top left); Minden Pictures/ Minden Pictures/ Superstock, pp. 8 (top center), 14-15; Malcolm Schuyl/ FLPA/ Glow Images, p. 8 (bottom); Tier und Naturfotografie/ Superstock, pp. 10-11; Reload Design, p. 11 (top left); injun, p. 11 (top right); Evgeniy Ayupov, p. 11 (middle left); Panachai Cherdchucheep, p. 11 (middle right); Melinda Fawver, p. 11 (bottom left, bottom right); Ullimi, p. 12; BIANCA LAVIES/ National Geographic Creative, pp. 12-13; Gerrit Vyn/ Nature Picture Library, p. 14; David M. Dennis/ Age Fotostock, pp. 16-17; PAULA COULTER/ Nature Picture Library, pp. 18-19, 19; Eric Isselee, p. 20 (top left); mlorenz, p. 20 (top right); Svetlana Foote, p. 20 (middle left); Ultrashock, p. 20 (middle right); Cynthia Kidwell, p. 20 (bottom left); vblinov, p. 20 (bottom right); Wayne Lynch/ Glow Images, pp. 20-21.